MW00957847

KNOW YOUR WORTH

365 INSPIRATIONAL QUOTES, TWEETS & POSTS FOR TEENAGE GIRLS

Know Your Worth

365 Inspirational Quotes, Tweets & Posts
for Teenage Girls

———————

Shawn McBride

Know Your Worth

Copyright © 2014 by (Shawn Maurice McBride)

All rights reserved. No part of this book may be reproduced or transmitted in any form or by any means without written permission from the author.

ISBN-13: **978-1495453939**
ISBN-10: **1495453936**

Dedication

This book is dedicated to the thousands upon thousands of teenage girls all across America that I have had the privilege of serving over the last two decades. I have learned from you by reading your letters, emails, tweets, posts, and text messages. You are loved! You are appreciated! You are valuable! You are special! May these words encourage you.

Shawn McBride Washington, DC
Winter 2014

TABLE OF CONTENTS

ATTITUDE
& BEAUTY

January 1

People who HATE themselves... LOVE to talk about other people!

#StayFocused
#IgnoreThem

January 2

Keep your head up b/c your CROWN might fall off! YOU ARE BEAUTIFUL, VALUABLE, & SPECIAL!

January 5

What u THINK
about, you BRING
about! Think
positive!

January 6

Never argue! Speak to those who listen. Walk away from those who don't!

January 3

A POSITIVE MINDSET is powerful in helping anyone accomplish their goals! You CAN do it!

January 4

Complaining
NEVER solves your
problems. You have
to actually DO
SOMETHING
about it.
#Get2Steppin
#NoExcuses
#MakeAPlan

January 7

My Selfish Friends:
I'm not an
astronomer, but
I'm pretty sure the
earth revolves
around the sun and
not YOU.
#StopSmellingYourself
#HelpOthers

January 8

1 Peter 3:3-4

Your beauty should not come from outward adornment... , Instead, it should be that of your inner self, the unfading beauty of a gentle and quiet spirit, which is of great worth in God's sight.

January 9

I may not be the prettiest, smartest, or strongest, but at least I'm ME and I don't pretend to be someone that I'm not meant to be.

January 10

A pretty face is nothing if you have an ugly heart.
#BeKind

January 11

Say to yourself
today:
I AM THE BOMB
DOT COM!

January 12

Few things are more beautiful and aesthetic than a female with CONFIDENCE. It is not CUTE, nor attractive to hear a female CURSING & COMPLAINING about her life.

January 13

What makes a female beautiful isn't just her looks, but rather the ATTITUDE she has behind it!
#SelfConfidence

January 14

Being pretty isn't enough! If u want others to know your worth... SHOW your worth. Prove how VALUABLE u r. Excel!

January 15

Wearing designer clothes can't cover a woman's insecurity just like a nice car can't shield a man's lack of drive! You are not defined by the label of your clothes.

January 16

You will never get to the TOP trying to get to the BOTTOM of what everybody has to say about you. Ignore Gossip.
#StayFocused
#BeDifferent
#IgnoreChatter
#TrustTheLord
#Soar

January 17

I would argue that there are really only two types of people: PESSIMISTIC people & OPTIMISTIC people. PESSIMISTIC people see difficulty in every opportunity. OPTIMISTIC people see opportunity in every difficulty.
#StayPositive
#ExpectTheBest
#DontWorry #Smile

January 18

You are beautiful
and extremely
valuable so SHINE
BRIGHT LIKE A
DIAMOND!
*Matthew 5:16 Let
your light shine...*

January 19

BElieve in
YOUrself!

January 20

If a person's personality and demeanor is not kind and beautiful, then their physical appearance really is of no value. Inner beauty is way more important than outer beauty. Be beautiful! Treat others the way you would want to be treated!

January 21

Be a girl with a MIND, a woman with an ATTITUDE, and a lady with CLASS.

January 22

You were made to be REAL, not to be perfect.

January 23

Do not conform any longer to the pattern of this world, but be transformed by the renewing of your mind. Romans 12:2 Change the way you think. Be positive! You are special!

January 24

Your attitude should be the same as that of Christ Jesus... Who made Himself nothing, taking the very nature of a servant.

Philippians 2:5, 7

Have a beautiful heart by serving others, just as Christ Jesus.

January 25

Do everything without complaining or arguing, so that you... shine like stars in the universe.
Philippians 2:14-15
Life is hard sometimes. Stand out from others by NOT complaining. Be beautiful!

January 26

Pay attention to
those around you.
If you see someone
who needs a friend,
be there for her!
Encourage those
around you daily.

January 27

We have different gifts, according to the grace given us.

Romans 12:6

What talent do you have much more of than others around you? Everybody has a 'much' and God expects you to use it to bless others! He gave it specifically to you! Discover your 'much' today!

January 28

Resist the urge to brag. Each person is special in his/her own way. God opposes the proud, but gives grace to the humble.

1 Peter 5:5

January 29

Do not deceive one another. Leviticus 19:11

Always tell the truth. Be a friend to someone's face AND behind their back.

January 30

Be the best YOU that you can be. You are a work in progress. Don't be so hard on yourself! Today, think of two things you love about yourself and two things you can improve on. Set a goal, and get to it!

January 31

Let love and faithfulness never leave you; bind them around your neck, write them on the tablet of your heart.
Proverbs 3:3

LOVE God and LOVE others!

How can you show God's love today?

CHARACTER

February 1

Appreciate those who love you... Help those who need you... Forgive those who hurt you... Forget those who leave you...

February 2

Before you go and criticize someone else, remember, you've got your own imperfections too.

February 3

Be careful who you pretend to be. You may forget who you are!

February 4

Gossip is NEVER cool! If u want 2 know information just ASK the person. If u didn't see it with your eyes or hear it with your ears then shhhhh!!!

February 5

It's simple... Never lie to someone who trusts you, and never trust someone who lies to you.

February 6

If you have a problem with me, tell me. Not everyone else.

February 7

Everybody needs AFFIRMATION & ENCOURAGEMENT. Build people up. NEVER tear them down. Life & death R N the power of the tongue!
Proverbs 18:21

February 8

Commitment is doing the thing you said you would do, long after the mood or feeling you said it in has left you! #StickToIt

February 9

Your character is who you are when nobody is looking. Be honorable.

February 10

You should never LOOK DOWN on anyone unless you are willing 2 help pull them UP!

February 11

Always B slooooooow 2 criticize but extremely fast 2 appreciate!

February 12

For My Friends Struggling With Jealousy: Just because someone has more followers than you, does not make them better. HITLER had millions of followers... Jesus had 12! #Perspective

February 13

Friends just BE YOURSELF! You have been created in the image of God. You are special, unique, and valuable. There is NO ONE ELSE like you. You are fearfully and wonderfully made! Don't be a COPY when you have been created as an ORIGINAL!

February 14

Please do not let today determine your VALUE or WORTH. Listen to me, YOU are more beautiful than a rose & YOU leave a stronger impression than perfume! The Lord loves YOU! Happy Valentine's Day!!

February 15

If u want 2 b left
alone then go
where u can b
alone. If u r out
amongst other
members of society
be social!
#Manners
#ByeTechnology

February 16

For My Risky Friends: 1 choice made n weakness could literally ruin your credibility, honor, respect, and trust!
#SelfControl

February 17

Friends, never ever complain about the things that YOU have the power to change, but YOU choose not to.
#CounterProductive

February 18

Be more concerned with your character than your reputation, because your character is what you really are, while your reputation is merely what others think you are.

February 19

You will never have people beside you if you think you are above them.
#BeHumble
#StayLow

February 20

Knowledge will give you power, but character respect.

February 21

I've discovered over the years that some people tell LIES to avoid losing someone or something. Other tell the TRUTH to avoid losing themselves! Strive to be a person of character & integrity!

February 22

Lord, use my life to add value to the lives of others. Grant me the right words and the strength to lift people up in a world where they are constantly being pulled down. In Jesus name, Amen!

February 23

Lord, today please help me not to follow FADS but to set TRENDS.
#BeDifferent
#DontFollowTheCrowd
#NonComformity
#OutOfTheBox

February 24

Dressing immodestly & inappropriately is like rolling around in MANURE. Truly, you will get a lot of attention, but mostly from PIGS! I'm just saying...

February 25

Racism ain't cool. Diversity is beautiful. I wish we could all be like my man, Super Mario... he was an Italian plumber, created by Japanese people, speaks English, but looks Hispanic!
John 3:16
For God so loved the world.
#LoveOneAnother

February 26

A competent and self-confident person is incapable of jealousy in anything. Jealousy is invariably a symptom of insecurity.
#BeConfident
#DontBeJelly

February 27

I was listening to the radio and heard a popular song by Frank Ocean. In the song, he asks an extremely important question: DO YOU NOT THINK SO FAR AHEAD? Yes, BINGO! Listen, this is PRECISELY what you must do to become successful in life: THINK FAR AHEAD. Before you make a major decision... THINK FAR AHEAD... Before you have sex with him THINK FAR AHEAD. Before you smoke that blunt or drink that alcohol, THINK FAR AHEAD. Don't put yourself in that situation! The choices & decisions you make TODAY will affect you TOMORROW, so THINK FAR AHEAD.

Proverbs 12:15 The way of a fool is right in his own eyes, but a wise man listens to advice.

February 28

Jealousy is simply
the fear that you do
not have value.
#Don'tFallForIt
#NotTrue

CHOICES

March 1

If you are in a dating relationship, you must BE CAREFUL to maintain your purity. Let me illustrate: Humpty Dumpty sat on a wall... Humpty Dumpty had a great fall... Uh Oh! Poor HUMPTY! My question is simple: Why was an EGG sitting on a wall? (Duh) I don't believe anything good happens when an egg tempts fate by climbing on a wall. Heights and breakable things don't mix, and neither do Christians & sexually compromising situations. I REST MY CASE! Be careful where you sit!

March 2

Friends, don't cry over the PAST, it's gone. Don't stress about the FUTURE, cause it hasn't arrived. Live in the present and make it beautiful.

March 3

No matter what the situation is, NEVER let your emotions overpower your intelligence.
Proverbs 25:28

#SelfControl
#KeepCalm
#BePatient

March 4

Learn to discern between a good thing and a God thing. Just because an opportunity presents itself, doesn't mean it's for you. Pray about it!

March 5

When you hear rumors or gossip, you can either add fuel to the fire or PUT IT OUT.

March 6

UNFRIEND, UNFOLLOW, DELETE, or just BLOCK the people who bring out the WORST in you. You deserve so much better!

March 7

NEVER allow social media, television, movies, music, Xbox1, PS4, Smart Phones, Apps, & other forms of entertainment & technology to hinder your relationship with the Lord. Forgive us for worshipping our manmade little gods that we have made into IDOLS. Forgive us for neglecting YOUR WORD & PRAYER. Help us to treat our Bibles like we treat our cell phones. *Hebrews 12:1 Lay aside EVERY WEIGHT THAT HINDERS...*

March 8

If we deliberately keep on sinning after we have received the knowledge of the truth, no sacrifice for sins is left, but only a fearful expectation of judgment and of raging fire that will consume the enemies of God... How much more severely do you think someone deserves to be punished who has trampled the Son of God underfoot... It is a dreadful thing to fall into the hands of the living God.

March 9

Being

MODEST

is the

HOTTEST!

March 10

1 John 3:9-10 No one born of God makes a practice of sinning... he cannot keep sinning because He has been born of God. This is the evidence of who are children of God, and children of the devil. Whoever does not practice righteousness is not born of God.

March 11

The Bible is a MIRROR to see your own sins not a WINDOW to see the sins of others. #FocusOnYourself

March 12

Your Business Ain't Butter, Stop Spreading It!

March 13

The ability to say "I'M SORRY" shows that we are able to see the other person's point of view, and that we want to maintain the relationship. It's amazing how many problems disappear once we decide to say "I'M SORRY."
#RichDevoss

March 14

For Frustrated People Only: U will never change what u tolerate.

March 15

If you decide to take a walk with someone, inevitably the person you are walking will adjust to your pace OR you will adjust to their pace. It happens unconsciously. Thus, be very careful with who you decide to WALK WITH. Be a STUDENT that sets the pace!

Proverbs 13:20 If you want to be wise, then WALK with the wise, he that WALKS with fools will suffer harm.

March 16

I realize that the weather is getting a little warmer, however showing a lot of skin is no way to find your Prince Charming. Prince Charming likes his gifts wrapped!

March 17

Be sure to surround yourself with people who show signs of GENIUS. Avoid people who show signs of STUPIDITY.

March 18

Proverbs 13:20

Hang with the wise and become wise; associate with fools and you will get in trouble.

March 19

Listen, I have encouraged many, many young girls over the years that a BAD relationship is exactly like a BAD movie... You won't leave because you keep hoping & believing the next scene will get BETTER!

#MoveOn #ShutItDown #YouDeserveBetter

March 20

For My Discouraged Friends: Commitment is doing the thing you said you would do -
– long after the mood or feeling you said it in has left you!

March 21

4 Teenage Girls Only: If you're not really interested in a dude then don't give him your personal contact info.

#JustSayNope
#NoWayJose
#SorryCharlie
#KnowYourWorth

March 22

FYI: The reason dudes keep calling you 'sexy' is because you keep showing by your pics that the only thing you have to offer is on the OUTSIDE, but not enough on the INSIDE. Take a pic of your BRAIN & a BOOK not your BUTT, BREASTS, or BOOTY! #KnowYourWorth

March 23

Relationship issues should be between TWO people, not two people plus ALL OF FACEBOOK or INSTAGRAM!

#Bdiscreet
#shhhh
#StopTellingYourBusiness

March 24

Life is a series of choices. The choices we make now affect the options available for the next round of choices.

March 25

For Teenage Girls Only: Don't be afraid of HEIGHTS... set your standards HIGH!
#RaiseTheBar
#BeHardToGet
#DontBeEasy

March 26

If you stay in a bad relationship, it will always HURT YOU. If you leave a bad relationship, it will hurt him!

March 27

The only way to get
a guy to stop
cheating on you is
by leaving him!
Respect yourself!
#KeepItMoving
#SayByeBye

March 28

In the words of BEYONCE in a recent interview with Oprah Winfrey: "Me and my husband, Sean Carter, were friends for a year and a half and only spoke on the phone before we ever went on our first date."

#SlowYourRoll
#PatienceIsAVirtue

March 29

In the words of Taylor Swift: I knew you were trouble when you walked in... shame on me now... *Proverbs 12:26 A righteous person is cautious in friendships...*

March 30

Life is not about you, but it is UP to you.

March 31

Always chase after the Lord and your dreams but never chase a boy... let 'em chase you!

COURAGE

April 1

Don't be afraid of HEIGHTS... set your standards HIGH!

April 2

Never be AFRAID
of being different!
Be AFRAID &
SCARED to death
to be just like
everybody else!

April 3

The sky is not the limit, your MIND is...

April 4

You are too GOOD of a person to be treated so BAD. Just because YOU are good for them, doesn't mean THEY are good for you!
Be brave. Walk away!

April 5

Lord, give me just enough friends to be affirmed, pain to stay humble, blessings to be thankful, & the courage of Caleb to go against the flow. Help me to follow Christ and not the crowd.

April 6

The first step to getting what you want is having the courage to get rid of what you don't.

April 7

Stand up for what is right. Have the courage to follow your heart, not the company you keep.

April 8

People don't talk about people who aren't doing anything significant. When people talk about you take it as a compliment! #StayFocused #BeStrong

April 9

Just because something is hard doesn't mean you shouldn't try it. It just means you should try harder.

April 10

The path to
success starts when
you stop fearing
yourself.
#GetOutOfYour
ComfortZone

April 11

Live your life as God directs you, for the worst mistake to make is to be afraid of failure, for failure comes with OPPORTUNITIES and windows of SUCCESS.

April 12

Ask yourself if
what you are doing
today is getting you
closer to where you
want to be
tomorrow.
#ChangeIt

April 13

It's not the broken dream that breaks our heart, but the dream we didn't dare to dream. Dream big! You can do anything you set your mind to do!

April 14

Hard days are the best because that's when champions are made. If you can push through the hard days, you can make it through anything.
-Gabby Douglas

April 15

MIRACLE is another word for EFFORT.
#BeBrave
#StepOut

April 16

When you are being picked on, remember that they are just trying to bring you down. You are better than what they say about you.

April 17

You never know
what you can really
do until you TRY.

April 18

There are so many people out there who will tell you that you can't make it. What you have to do is turn around and say, "Watch me".

April 19

Confidence and faith in God are the most important things needed to fulfill your dreams. Begin to live your dreams from today; tomorrow is too late.

April 20

It's easier to become a matching wing to a butterfly than the crystal of a snowflake.

April 21

Keep your head up, don't you give up! No matter what obstacles you may face, you must always finish the race.

April 22

You are the designer of your destiny. You are the author. You write the story, the pen is in your hand and the outcome is whatever you choose. Just remember three sentences whenever life puts you in difficulties: I CAN DO IT, I WILL DO IT, AND I WILL PROVE IT!!! That's it. Every successful person has a painful story, every painful person has a successful ending, accept the pain and get ready for success!!! Let's go!!!

April 23

Learn from your past, work hard in the present, and you will taste success in the future.

April 24

Faith is taking the first step, even when you can't see the whole staircase.
#BeDifferent
#FollowYourDream

April 25

Don't take a path;
leave a trail. Lead;
don't follow.

April 26

The first step to success is saying you WILL succeed.

April 27

If I can shine
without diamonds,
then I can soar
without wings.

April 28

You hit what you
aim at! If you aim
at nothing, you will
hit it every time.
Set a goal today!

April 29

It is not up to
anyone to say you
can't, but YOU to
say I CAN.

April 30

Let others say what they want, because it doesn't mean anything unless YOU LET IT mean something.

DATING & DUDES

May 1

Realize that the best marriages are based on long FRIENDSHIPS. Take it slow...

May 2

In my opinion no respectable guy of character wants to date a girl who dresses like she's on the menu and available for TAKE OUT!
#KnowYourWorth
#ValueYourself
#PutOnClothes

May 3

You should never
RUSH that which
you want to last!
#BePatient

May 4

The better person
you become, the
better person you
will attract.

May 5

A BOY will tell U that he loves U but a REAL MALE will show U. Love is a verb. Actions speak LOUDER than words.

May 6

Never chase a dude. Your beautiful LIGHT that comes from your connection to Christ will cause dudes to pursue you. In the words of Rihanna: SHINE BRIGHT LIKE A DIAMOND!

May 7

Don't let the fact that he is CUTE make you ignore the fact that he is CRAZY!
#Discern

May 8

Don't fall in love
with who you
THINK they are
when you still don't
know WHO they
actually are!

May 9

Never chase a boy.
Let him find you
and realize your
worth!

May 10

Be careful about going over to his house JUST TO WATCH A MOVIE!! Are you kidding me? #BeenThere #DoneThat #BeSmart!

May 11

If God is not in your relationship, you shouldn't be either.
#Get2steppin

May 12

Stop RUNNING
after the dudes
whom you need to
WALK away from!
#BewareOfBadCompany
Being single is
better than being
in a bad
relationship.

May 13

ALWAYS let a boy pursue YOU! Don't get it twisted. Never and I mean never chase after a boy. A boy will eventually lose respect for a DESPERATE girl.
#Wait
#BePatient

May 14

Never get jealous when you see you exboyfriend with someone else, because my parents always taught me to give my used toys to the less fortunate.

May 15

Please stop making excuses for immature males who are just plain PATHETIC! If he doesn't add value to your life, he needs to be subtracted!

#MathematicalDiscernment

May 16

If you're not really interested in a dude, then don't give him your personal contact info.
#JustSayNope
#NoWayJose
#SorryCharlie
#KnowYourWorth

May 17

Honestly U deserve someone who will JUMP FENCES 2 B w/u not someone who is ON THE FENCE about being with U.

May 18

There is a HUGE difference between LOVE & LUST. Never get this twisted. Listen, if a guy is pressuring you to sleep with him OR to send him seductive pictures of you, then read my words very carefully:
THAT AIN'T LOVE SWEETIE!

May 19

Each and every MALE on earth has flaws, period. Instead of looking for a MALE who is PERFECT look for the one who is PERFECT for you!
#ThatsMuchBetter #Logic

May 20

Unfortunately some girls pick perfume how they pick a guy... a cute bottle BUT watered down content!

May 21

You must learn to distinguish between a male who FLATTERS you and a male who COMPLIMENTS you... a male who SPENDS money on you and a male who INVESTS in you... a male who views you as PROPERTY and a male who views you PROPERLY... a male who LUSTS after you and a male who LOVES you. A male who views you as his TROPHY and a male who views you as his TREASURE!

May 22

If u r dating someone & YOU ARGUE & FIGHT more than you ENJOY BEING TOGETHER that's a sign that u should seriously consider calling it quits & in the words of Taylor Swift: "Never ever ever get back together." Like ever!

May 23

One guy can love a million girls in one way but it takes a real man to love one girl for a million reasons.

May 24

Friends, relationship issues should be between TWO people, not two people plus ALL OF FACEBOOK!

#BeDiscreet
#shhhh
#StopTellingYourBusiness

May 25

Listen up: Just because you are a teen, does not mean that a boyfriend is a requirement! Don't rush. God has chosen someone just for you and He will send him to you when He is ready. #GodsTimeline

May 26

Be Encouraged!
The relationship
had to end because
God was
PROTECTING
YOU from less than
His best.
#StayFocused
#YouWillSee

May 27

So y'all broke up, huh? Don't cry because it's over, smile because it happened. Listen, you are not a VICTIM! Who you are & who you will become in life is your responsibility... *Romans 8:31 If God be for us, who can be against us?* Stop making excuses & pleeeze stop smoking the addictive drug of self-pity... GET OVER IT! Move on with your life! In the famous words of Sean Carter... On to the next one!

May 28

So you think a boy is cute? Check his morals and his actions, sweetie. He won't be cute when he's locked up or he's cheating on you!

May 29

There is a difference between being INTERESTED in someone and COMMITTED to someone.

May 30

Don't get it twisted sweetheart... If your boyfriend really misses you HE WILL call or text you. If he cares deeply about you HE WILL show it. If not, he cannot be worth your time because CLEARLY you are not worth his. Keep it moving!

May 31

Smart girls open their minds, easy girls open their legs, and foolish girls open their hearts.

FORGIVENESS

June 1

FORGIVENESS clears you of having to worry about how to punish the person who hurt you. When you choose to FORGIVE someone you are not turning them loose, rather you are turning them over to God. FORGIVE & be free. Let it go!

June 2

If you are in a relationship with another human being, they will hurt you, whether intentionally or unintentionally. How should you respond? Always use the "F" WORD. FORGIVE! That's really why Jesus came into the world... to offer the "F" Word to sinners like you and me! *Ephesians 4:32 FORGIVE each other, just as... Christ FORGAVE you.*

June 3

Hurt People… Hurt People thus FORGIVENESS is the only solution. Let it go! *Matthew 6:12 FORGIVE us of our trespasses even as we FORGIVE those who have trespassed against us.* Twitter: @shawnmcbride74

June 4

You will never truly understand how strong your heart is until you can finally forgive the person that broke it.
#LetItGo

June 5

God calls on us to
forgive, but that
doesn't mean you
have to forget.
Don't make the
same mistake
twice.

June 6

Great relationships are not created by people who never hurt each other, only by the people who choose to keep 'no record of wrong'.
1 Corinthians 13:5
Love keeps NO RECORD OF WRONG.

June 7

Resentment, bitterness & anger are very self-destructive and counterproductive. They will never solve the real problem. The only solution to our hurts is FORGIVENESS.

Job 5:2 (GN) To worry yourself to death with resentment would be a foolish and senseless thing to do.

June 8

Research has proven that the 3 most destructive emotions are resentment, bitterness, & unforgiveness. When you choose to hold on to this trio, you hurt yourself emotionally & physically. *Job 21:23-25 (GN) Some men stay healthy until the day they die...others have no happiness at all; they live and die with bitter hearts.*

June 9

Forgiving someone who hurt you or betrayed you is not minimizing the seriousness of the offense against you. Forgiveness is not saying "It was no big deal!", or "It didn't hurt!" No! What happened to you was a big deal and it did hurt. You were wounded and you were wronged. Unforgiveness is a choice to stay bitter; forgiveness is a choice to get better.

June 10

Forgiving a person
who has hurt you or
betrayed you does not
mean that you will
instantly trust them.
Forgiveness is an
instant act, but Trust
must be rebuilt over a
period of time. The
person who hurt you
or betrayed you must
develop a new track
record.

June 11

Forgiveness means that I will let go of the hurt. Hurt People... Hurt People thus FORGIVENESS is the only solution. Let it go! *Matthew 6:12 FORGIVE us of our trespasses even as we FORGIVE those who have trespassed against us.* It is what I am obligated to do. The person who hurt me has an obligation to seek to earn trust over a period of time.

June 12

Forgiveness is not resuming the relationship without any changes. Just because you forgive someone who hurt you DOES NOT MEAN you must accept the person back into your life just the way they were & let them continue to hurt you.

June 11

After you forgive someone, if the relationship is to be restored the person who hurt you (offender) must do three things: REPENT, offer RESTITUTION, and REBUILD your trust over a period of time.

June 12

Forgiveness is a two way street. You cannot receive from the Lord what you are unwilling to give to others. What you sow, you will also reap. If you refuse to forgive you are burning the very bridge you will eventually need to walk across. Let It Go! *Matthew 6:15 If you do not forgive others, then your Father will not forgive the wrongs you have done.*

June 13

One practical reason to forgive someone who has hurt or betrayed you is simply because God has forgiven you. Father God through Christ Jesus our Lord has wiped your slate clean. All of the things you deserve to be paid back for from God will not be paid back because God has wiped the slate clean. You will never have to forgive anybody more than God has already forgiven you. *Daniel 9:9 (NLT) But the Lord, our God, is merciful and forgiving, even though we have rebelled against him. Ephesians 1:7 NLV Because of the blood of Christ, we are bought and made free from the punishment of sin. And because of His blood, our sins are forgiven...*

June 14

Forgiveness should be somewhat easy to grant an offender when we recognize that we ALL ARE IMPERFECT HUMAN BEINGS. *Ecclesiastes 7:20* reminds us that there is not a single person in all the earth who is always good and never sins.

June 15

Before you decide to write someone off as UNFORGIVABLE u must 1st take a good look at yourself in the mirror. You are human too & are just as capable of hurting or betraying someone.

June 16

Why Should You Forgive Someone Who Has Hurt You? (1) *Romans 3:10 As it is written, There is none righteous, no, not one. (2) Romans 3:23 For all have sinned, and come short of the glory of God. (3) Because we're all capable of hurting others. To err is human, but to forgive is divine.*
Let It Go!

June 17

The best thing you can do about someone who has hurt or betrayed you in the past is to FORGIVE them. Why? So you can be FREE. Stop letting people from your past continue to hurt you in the present. In my Kanye West voice: "No One Person Should Have All That Power!" Forgive & be free! *Romans 12:19 Never avenge yourselves. Leave that to God, for He has said that He will repay those who deserve it.*

June 18

If we are to forgive someone for their hurt/pain caused to us we must ABANDON OUR RIGHT TO GET EVEN. Sounds unfair? It is. I can't find any Scriptures where God promised that this life would be fair. Let It Go!

June 19

How do you know when you've FULLY FORGIVEN someone of the hurt/pain they have caused? Answer: When you can, with the help of the Lord, do these 3 things: *Luke 6:27-28...* *Do GOOD* to those who hate you, BLESS those who curse you, and PRAY FOR those who mistreat you.

June 20

Pastor Shawn, how do I FORGIVE someone who has hurt & betrayed me? (1) Stop focusing on them (2) Stop focusing on what they did. But, why? Because as long as you continue to focus on that person they control you... FORGIVE & Let It Go!

June 21

4MyDiscouraged Friends: When people don't really know u or understand u they will either criticize u or gossip about u. #StayFocused #Ignore

June 22

The ability to say "I'M SORRY" shows that we are able to see the other person's point of view, that we want to maintain the relationship... it's amazing how many problems disappear once we decide to say "I'M SORRY."
#RichDevoss

June 23

If they can't repent to GOD... they can never apologize to you!
#MoveOn
#Forgive
#TheirProblemIsNotReallyYou

June 24

Forgiving isn't about what it does for someone else, it's about what it does for YOU!

June 25

Don't forgive people because you are weak. Forgive them because you are strong enough to realize the fact that people make mistakes. Forgive as Christ forgave you...

June 26

Forgiving someone, whether it is your best friend, your boyfriend, or your parents is almost never easy. Do it anyway.
#LifeIsNotEasy

June 27

To forgive is to set
a prisoner free &
discover that the
prisoner was you.

June 28

People gonna hate you, rate you, and try to break you, but how strong you stand - that's what makes you, YOU.
#Ignore
#WalkAwayandForgetIt

June 29

To be a Christian is to forgive the inexcusable because God has forgiven the inexcusable in you.

June 30

The truth is, unless you let go, unless you forgive yourself, unless you forgive the situation, unless you realize that the situation is over, you cannot move forward."

KNOW YOUR
WORTH!

July 1

Instead of wishing you were someone else, be proud of who you are. You never know who was looking at you wishing they were you.

July 2

You might feel worthless to one person, but you are priceless to another. Don't ever forget your value.

July 3

Nothing is sexier
than a girl with
confidence. We
don't think it's cute
to hear you
complain about
your life.

July 4

You are not a Facebook status... stop waiting around for people to like you. *Psalm 139:14 U R fearfully & wonderfully made.*

July 5

Say "NO" 2 low self-esteem! You are too valuable to think low of yourself.

July 6

Stop allowing INSECURE ppl 2 keep u down!

July 7

You don't deserve better if you don't expect & demand better! Raise the bar!

July 8

I've learned over the years from speaking & listening to thousands & thousands of teenage girls that the more you VALUE YOURSELF, the more you will be VALUED BY OTHERS. Psalm 139:14 You are wonderfully made... #KnowYourValue If YOU don't believe in YOU who will?

July 9

For My Discouraged Friends: You have an SEA of potential don't drown in a small puddle of criticism!
#StayFocused

July 10

People who HATE themselves... LOVE to talk about other people!
#StayFocused

July 11

What YOU allow is
exactly what will
continue until YOU
stop allowing it.
#ItsNotRocketScience

July 12

If you love someone and that person rejects you, don't curse your fate. It's THEIR loss that they didn't love you.Let it remind you there's someone more lucky in the world, who deserves your love.

July 13

Believe in yourself.
Have faith in your
abilities. Remind
yourself that God is
with you and
nothing can defeat
you!

July 14

You can only be as
good as the goals
you set for yourself.
If you let God be
your light and
follow your
dreams, you will
never fail.

July 15

No matter how hard it is to achieve my dream, I'll put in all my effort and do my best! Dreams come true for those who really work hard. Don't give up easily!

July 16

"No child is born a mistake, just an unexpected miracle."

July 17

Everyone has a
special quality.
Find it in you and
go for it as soon as
possible.
#NoExcuses
#YouAreUnique

July 18

Always believe in yourself. No matter who's around you being negative or thrusting negative energy, totally block it off. Cause whatever believe, you become.
-Michael Jackson

July 19

Don't say, 'No one likes Me.' Just say, 'There is no one like Me.' - Attitude matters.

July 20

Do not be a victim of negative self-talk. Remember, you are listening.

July 21

You aren't your looks, or your gender, or your weight. You are not where you were born or who your parents are. You aren't always who you want to be. You are what you do in life and who you help. You are the legacy you are making and leave behind one day. You are what you do in this life you were given. Don't let people judge you on the things you aren't, let them see who you are.

July 22

You are the average of the 5 people you spend the most time with.
#ChooseWisely
#SeekExcellence
#ElevateYourself

July 23

If I take care of my character, my reputation will take care of itself.

July 24

You're one in a million... whatever you've been told, you're worth more than gold... of all the stars out tonight, you shine brighter... so don't be ashamed to wear your crown, you're a king, you're a queen inside and out.

July 25

When life seems rough, just keep your head held high. You are more capable than you give yourself credit for. Don't belittle your accomplishments because they matter and so do you.

July 26

Ladies, those models on magazines and TV, that's FAKE and AIRBRUSHED beauty. The image you see in the mirror every morning, that's REAL beauty that's made from GOD.

July 27

Never compare yourself with others. God made only one YOU. You are unique and special!

July 28

Every soul has a purpose. Every life has a meaning. So what's yours?

July 29

Talent does not search for the person, in fact the person needs to search for the talent inside him and take it out to show the world.

July 30

Whatever you say you are is what you become so say: "I AM A WINNER."

July 31

Everything you need is right inside of you. It's there waiting for you to unlock it. Within you is goodness, truth, love and light.

SUCCESS

&

PERSISTENCE

August 1

If you don't like the
way something is,
change it.
Complaining and
constant negativity
aren't going to fix
it.
Comfort is the
enemy of
achievement!

August 2

For Smart Teenagers Only: If some people are calling you a NERD today don't worry cause they will be calling you BOSS tomorrow!
#Stayfocused
#Work&StudyHard

August 3

Breaking News: Successful people are not ONLY gifted, rather they just WORK HARD, then succeed on purpose! *Proverbs 14:23*

August 4

Stop being afraid of what could go wrong. And start being positive about what could go right.

August 5

Shoot for the TOP because the BOTTOM is too over crowded. The sky is NOT the limit. That is NONSENSE! Why reach LOW for the stars when you can aim HIGH for the moon? *Matthew 19:26 With God... ALL THINGS ARE POSSIBLE.*

August 6

Information without application is only fascination. Information with application leads to transformation.

August 7

3 keys to your success in life: Work while others R loafing; prepare while others R playing; dream while others R wishing.
#SuccessSecrets

August 8

The truth is not everyone will be happy about your success! Just accept it. Some people are hoping, praying, and wishing that you fail! Stay focused on GOD and your GOALS! *Genesis 50:20 You intended to harm me...*

August 9

Actually I started becoming successful when I changed my PERSONAL PHILOSOPHY. In other words, for your life to really change YOU must change. YOU may not be able to change an election but YOU sure can change YOURSELF.

August 10

Never ask the Lord to make your life easier, instead ask Him to make YOU better.

August 11

Whatever you FOCUS on the LONGEST becomes the STRONGEST!

August 12

Most Christians are
not in imminent
danger of loosing
theirs lives... they
are facing a danger
that's far worse:
WASTING IT!

August 13

We really believe
that God can do
greater things in
our lives but we
just crop ourselves
out of the picture.

August 14

If you want to be successful in this life that has been graciously given to you by the Lord you must BUILD A CHAMPIONSHIP TEAM AROUND YOU. Surround yourself with people who want to HELP you, not HURT or HINDER you. Your starting line up must be tight! *Proverbs 13:20*

August 15

Do you set goals? I do! I achieved my 1st major goal at age 16 when I saved $400 & purchased my 1st car. I was sooo PSYCHED! Lol! One reason I love setting GOALS is because over the years GOALS always seem to ENTICE ME to become the person it takes to achieve them. Listen friends, I have discovered over the last 20 years that many people fail in life NOT because they AIM TOO HIGH & MISS rather they AIM TOO LOW & HIT. Never set your goals too low because if you don't aim @ much you will NEVER achieve much. This verse should inspire you:

Matthew 19:26With God ALL THINGS ARE POSSIBLE.

August 16

Plans go wrong for lack of advice; many advisers will bring much success.

August 17

EXCUSES are the nails that you use when you are trying to build a house of FAILURE.

August 18

Words of Wisdom
from *Ecclesiastes*

11:9-12:1

1. Enjoy Life & Always Have Fun.

2. Live Responsibly

3. Get Help for Your Emotional Problems

 4. Stay Far Away From Evil

5. Remember Your Creator.

August 19

Replace excuses
with effort.

August 20

Replace laziness with determination.

August 21

U will never know how strong U really R until being strong is the ONLY option U have. Don't give up!

August 22

Sometimes you must talk yourself OUT OF doubt and INTO faith.
#YesYouCan

August 23

B4 u give up take a
moment to think
about why u held
on 4 so long.
#KeepHoldingOn

August 24

Friends, Never ever
complain about the
things that YOU
have the power to
change but YOU
choose not to.
#CounterProductive

August 25

BE PATIENT!
Anything of value
that is worth
having takes TIME!

August 26

For My Frustrated Friends: When U stop caring about what certain people think about U then and only them your life will begin to soar like an eagle!
#BewareofBadCompany

August 27

For Smart Teenagers Only: If some people are calling you a NERD today don't worry cause they will be calling you BOSS tomorrow!
#Stayfocused
#Work&StudyHard

August 28

Breaking News: Successful people are not ONLY gifted, rather they just WORK HARD, then succeed on purpose! *Proverbs 14:23*

August 29

People who are crazy enough to believe they can change the world... usually do! GO CRAZY!

August 30

The poorest man is not one without money – it's a man without a dream!

August 31

For Teenagers Only: School is not a CIRCUS so don't act like a CLOWN... Work hard & stay focused... Your future depends on you!

WHEN LIFE GIVES YOU LEMONS... BE PERSISTENT. DON'T GIVE UP!

September 1

Sometimes the Lord doesn't want to give you something you want, not because you don't deserve it, but because you deserve more.

September 2

In life things don't happen for no reason, they happen to teach you something.

September 3

Your relationship ended. Not your life.

September 4

Adversity is life's disappointments & difficulties. It is the hardships, misfortunes, setbacks, sorrows & painful experiences that we ALL face sooner or later. When adversity comes to you, will you crack or will you allow the fires of adversity to be your teacher and thus engage you in a process of transforming you into who we are meant to become.

September 5

Forget your past...
Yesterday is
history. Tomorrow
is a mystery. Today
is a gift. That's why
it's called the
present.

September 6

Friends, the difficult PROBLEMS that we face in life are not the END of the road just a BEND in the road. Eventually things will straighten out for you. How do I know this? Because NO SEASON LASTS FOREVER. Today trust the Lord. He is with you. This too shall pass. NO SEASON LASTS FOREVER. *Isaiah 43:2 When you go through deep waters, I will be with you. When you go through rivers of difficulty, you will not drown...*

September 7

Psalm 61:2... I cry to you for help when my heart is overwhelmed. Lead me...

September 8

PATIENCE is a virtue. Just because something isn't happening to you right now, doesn't mean that will never happen.

September 9

You are NOT what you are going through! This too shall pass!

September 10

Stress will make you believe that everything has to happen right now but FAITH reassures you that everything will all work out in God's timing.
#BePatient

September 11

There will be times in our lives when we don't understand why God is allowing certain things to happen. Be Encouraged & Trust that He knows what He is doing. Think on this: *Isaiah 55:8-9 My thoughts are nothing like your thoughts, says the Lord, and my ways are far beyond anything you could imagine. For just as the heavens are higher than the earth, so my ways are higher than your ways...*
Newlifebowie.com

September 12

It will all work out in the end and if it hasn't worked out, it means it's not the end yet!

September 13

I challenge you to stop asking God to TAKE AWAY our PROBLEMS, rather to ask Him for PERSEVERANCE instead.

September 14

Friends, the difficult PROBLEMS, OBSTACLES & CHALLENGES that are STRETCHING you today are actually STRENGTHENING you for tomorrow. Be encouraged and don't give up on GOD or your GOALS. *Hebrews 11:27 By faith Moses... PERSEVERED because he saw HIM who is invisible.*

September 15

Keep your head LOOKING UP today because if you are LOOKING DOWN you won't be able to see ALL of the BLESSINGS that the Lord has placed in your life. Things could be worse. The STORM will eventually pass. *Psalm 121:1-2 I lift up my eyes to the mountains... My help comes from the Lord, the Maker of heaven and earth.*

September 16

Today do not
confuse your
FEELINGS for
FACTS. Just because
you FEEL like a
FAILURE doesn't
mean you are one.
Keep moving
FORWARD. Be
encouraged!

September 17

Pain makes you stronger. Tears make you braver. Heartbreak makes you wiser. So thank the past for a better future.

September 18

What hurts you today will make you stronger tomorrow. Hold on!

September 19

Only YOU can choose to let your problems define u, confine u, refine u, outshine u... or YOU can move on & leave it all BEHIND YOU!

September 20

Today I only want to make improvements, not excuses.

September 21

For My Hurting Friends: Today do not confuse your FEELINGS for FACTS. Just because you FEEL like a FAILURE doesn't mean you are one. Keep moving FORWARD. Be encouraged!

September 22

Being single is better than being in a bad relationship.
#DatingIsAnOption

September 23

For My Frustrated Friends: Social Media is the WORST PLACE to come and tell ALL of your personal business. Find someone you can confide in PRIVATELY.

September 24

Heavenly Father today please be a fence all around me, assign angels over me, let goodness & mercy follow me and put real friends beside me. Cause every weapon formed against me to lose ammunition, take the bullseye off my back & help me reach my target. HELP ME to HELP OTHERS!

September 25

ONLY 4 things can change your life:
1) Do MORE of something
2) Do LESS of something
3) START something
4) STOP something

September 26

For My Discouraged Friends: Never focus on what you are going THROUGH but what you are going TO... #ThisTooShallPass #TheStormWillEndSo on #TheLordIsWithYou

September 27

Everything in life is temporary, if things are going good, enjoy it, if things are going bad, don't worry, it won't last forever either.

September 28

Always keep your head up, cause if it's down you won't be able to see the blessings that have been placed in your life.

September 29

Just because something isn't happening to you right now, doesn't mean that will never happen.

September 30

Self-pity is easily the most destructive of the non-pharmaceutical narcotics; it is addictive, gives momentary pleasure and separates the victim from reality. #Chinup

LEAN...on your FAITH and your PARENTS!

October 1

The quality of your life and the length of your life is determined by HOW YOU TREAT YOUR PARENTS...
Be respectful!
Here's proof: *Ephesians 6:2-3 Honor your father and mother which is the first commandment with a promise so that IT MAY GO WELL WITH YOU and that YOU MAY ENJOY LONG LIFE ON THE EARTH.*

October 2

... listen to your father's teaching and do not forget your mother's advice. Their teaching will be like flowers in your hair or a necklace around your neck.
(Proverbs 1:7-9)

October 3

Be quiet, Be humble & Be submissive to the authority of your parents. It's not GIVING UP it's called GROWING UP.

October 4

Your parents are now old & wise because they use to be YOUNG & STUPID!
#Listen
#BeenThereDoneThat

October 5

When you are the one who is wrong YOU lose the right to be angry! Be quiet, Be humble & Be submissive to the authority of your parents.

October 6

*Philippians 4:6...
Never worry about
anything. Instead,
in every situation
let your petitions
be made known to
God through
prayers and
requests, with
thanksgiving...*

October 7

Gives us clean hands give us pure hearts... let us not lift our souls up to another... Oh God let us be a GENERATION that seeks YOUR face...

October 8

Arguably the three most important words in the entire Bible. Read them very slowly: GOD IS ABLE. (Ephesians 3:20 & 2Corinthians 9:8)

October 9

Ask the Lord to help you today to do ordinary things extraordinarily well.

October 10

Happiness keeps you sweet. Trials keep you strong. Sorrows keep you human. Failures keep you humble. And God, keeps you going *Proverbs 3:5... In all of your ways acknowledge HIM and HE will direct your paths.*

October 11

The issue is not UNANSWERED prayer, rather it is UNOFFERED prayer. How can God ever ANSWER if we don't ASK? The Lord did not say "Call Me Maybe" *James 4:2 You have not because you ask not.*

—

October 12

*Hebrews 10:19-23...
because of the blood of
Jesus we can now
confidently go into the
holy place... We have
been sprinkled with his
blood to free us from a
guilty conscience... So
we must continue to
come to him with a
sincere heart & strong
faith... We must
continue to hold firmly
to our declaration of
faith.*

October 13

God doesn't move in your life when you struggle; He moves when you pray.

October 14

In order to GET
you must ASK
*James 4... u gave
not because you
ask not.*

October 15

I will walk by faith
even when I cannot
see because this
broken road prepares
Your will for me. Help
me to win my endless
fears You've been so
faithful for all my
years With the one
breath You make me
Your grace covers all I
do... (Jeremy Camp)

October 16

It's hard 4 certain people 2 believe what the Holy Spirit said to YOU simply because THEY did not hear Him. YOU did. He spoke to YOU.
#TakeAction

October 17

Just because God is
moving SLOW
does not mean the
answer is NO!
#BePatient

October 18

We can't see the WI-FI connection in our homes yet we trust that connection to our computers, iPads, etc. So why don't you put the very same trust in God for your lives that he will do what he says? It is called Faith... the connection you can't see but know it can and will happen!!! I'm a believer ;-)) #HesAble

October 19

As you waste your breath complaining about life, Someone out there is breathing their last. Appreciate what you have...

October 20

Thank God for another day. Don't waste it.

October 21

For Arrogant People w/SWAG Only: The life you live, the talents you possess and the gifts you have received are not simply personal accomplishments; Rather they are expressions of GOD's GRACE ON YOUR LIFE. Never, and I mean NEVER, take credit for what your Heavenly Father has provided & GRACIOUSLY done for you. Always Thank HIM & praise HIM 1st. *James 4:6 God opposes the proud but favors the humble.*

October 22

No! It's NOT too
good to be true...
it's happening to
the right person...
YOU! Stay positive,
celebrate & be
THANKFUL for
your blessings.

October 23

A life without the Lord is like an unsharpened pencil. It has no point!

October 24

Note 2 Self: Trusting the Lord is never easy. Perhaps the Lord has been waiting on YOU to CLOSE/END some things before He OPENS/BEGINS some things. Live by FAITH not FEAR! Hebrews 11:6 Without faith it's impossible to please God.

October 25

If you put The Lord first you will never come in second!

October 26

Indescribable, uncontainable, You placed the stars in the sky and You know them by name. You are amazing God... All powerful, untamable. Awestruck we fall to our knees as we humbly proclaim You are amazing God...

October 27

Sometimes you don't appreciate what you have because you're too focused on what you want.

October 28

There is an expiration date on blaming your parents for steering you in the wrong direction. The moment you are old enough to take the wheel, the responsibility lies with you.

October 29

Always suppress
your pride and
admit your wrong
for every
wrongdoing,
there's a chance to
learn the right
thing.

October 30

Never forget who you are and where you come from! It's an important part of you that you will find strength and peace from.

October 31

Slow down and find time to LISTEN to God. *I will instruct you and teach you in the way you should go. I will counsel you and watch over you. Psalm 32:8*

RELATIONSHIPS

November 1

NEVER ACKNOWLEDGE YOUR HATERS! The most simple way to deal with a hater is not to deal with them at all. They possess a negative aura around them and it may rub off on you if you're around them to long, so let a hater do their job, drink HATERAID! You are waaaaaaaaay too intelligent, beautiful & successful to waste time addressing haters. Stay focused & be successful!

November 2

Haters will broadcast your failure, but whisper your success...

November 3

When you're mad at someone you love, be careful what you say because your mind gets angry but your heart still cares.

November 4

EMBRACE only the people who bring out the BEST in you. It always makes SENSE to connect with people who have SENSE!

November 5

A BEST friend
scolds you like a
dad, cares like a
mom, teases like a
sister, irritates like
a brother, and
loves you more
than a lover.

November 6

Math was my favorite class when I was in school. Math really caused my brain to think & EVALUATE numbers carefully. Here's an assignment: Evaluate the friends in your life: Are your friends ADDING value to your life? Are your friends SUBTRACTING value from your life? Are your friends DIVIDING you? Are your friends MULTIPLYING you? Choose your friends carefully! *Proverbs 13:20 Whoever walks with the wise becomes wise, but the companion of fools will suffer harm.*

November 7

Select friends for your LIFETIME not just your TIMELINE.

#BewareOfBadCompany

November 8

*Proverbs 26:4
When arguing with fools, don't answer their foolish arguments, or you will become as foolish as they are.*

November 9

A real friend is happy for you even when your success doesn't involve them!!!

November
10

I speak to thousands of young girls every year. Here is one thing I have finally come to realize. Take heed: The reason that other girls are talking about you BEHIND your back is simply because YOU ARE IN FRONT OF THEM. Stay Focused on God & your Goals! Don't look back!

November 11

People too weak to follow their own dreams, will always find a way to discourage yours.

November 12

If you cannot CHANGE the people around you then CHANGE the people around you. *Proverbs 12:26 A righteous person is cautious in friendship.*

November 13

You become like the five people whom you spend the most time with. Choose wisely!

November 14

You don't have
time to hate people
who hate you cause
you should be too
busy loving people
who love you.

November 15

Say NO to DRAMA! The Lord made 1 universe, 8 planets, 204 countries, 804 islands, 7 seas, & 7 billion people. Please don't let 1 PERSON ruin your night!!! Stay focused!

November 16

When people don't really know u or understand u they will either criticize u or gossip about u. #StayFocused #Ignore

November 17

When people come into your life they not only bring their BODY but they also bring their SPIRIT. This is why *Proverbs 12:26* warns us to be CAUTIOUS in friendships.

November 18

Whenever a person who is seeking to live for the Lord gets deeply connected to people who do not have the same desire, it is not a good thing! Friends, be very CAUTIOUS when deciding who will get close to you!

November 19

Don't expect to see positive changes in your life if you surround yourself with negative people.

November 20

You don't need
anybody that
doesn't need you.
Focus on those
who truly
appreciate you and
get rid of those
who don't.

November 21

Before you ask
someone why they
hate you, ask
yourself why you
even care.

November 22

If you decide to take a walk with someone inevitably the person you are walking will adjust to your pace OR you will adjust to their pace. It happens unconsciously. Thus, be very careful with who you decide to WALK WITH this school year. Be a STUDENT that sets the pace! *Proverbs 13:20 If you want to be wise then WALK with the wise, he that WALKS with fools will suffer harm.*

November 23

A best friend knows you're sad; a best friend knows you're mad; a best friend knows you're crying; a best friend knows you're lying.

November 24

Life is not about
the people who act
true to your face.
It's about the
people who remain
true BEHIND
YOUR BACK.

November 25

Some people make your laugh a little louder, your smile a little brighter and your life a little better. They're the ones worth hanging onto.

November 26

For Teenage Girls Only: Listen,
when you discover that other
females are gossiping about YOU...
Never get mad; never get even;
simply GET AHEAD! GETTING
AHEAD, staying focused on your
goals, your dreams, and the purpose
the Lord has for your life is always
the best revenge. Harness your
ANGER to become massively
successful and you will eventually
silence all of your haters & critics.
This world is too BIG for YOU and
opportunities are too VAST to waste
YOUR precious time responding to
& focusing on people with small
minds. YOU must be special If
people are always talking about
YOU. Be encouraged today!
*Proverbs 16:32 Whoever is slow to
ANGER is better than the mighty,
and he who rules his spirit than he
who takes a city.*

November 27

While you may not be BETTER than anybody else... some people can make you WORSE! The Law of Association: You become like the people you hang around.

November 28

GOSSIPING is not cool or cute. It makes you look very unattractive. If you have a problem with another girl tell HER, NOT everyone else.

November 29

Listen, if you didn't see it with YOUR OWN eyes or hear it with YOUR OWN ears, then always mind YOUR OWN business. *Proverbs 11:13*

November 30

Let go of those who
bring you down
and surround
yourself with those
who bring out the
best in you.

QUOTES
FOR LIFE

December 1

Thank you Lord for strategically placing my eyes IN FRONT of my head... Keep me from LOOKING BACK!

December 2

Be encouraged friends! I've discovered over the years of my life that sometimes you must go through the worst, in order to get to the best.
#Process
#Patience

December 3

Only YOU can choose to let your problems define u, confine u, refine u, outshine u... or YOU can move on & leave it all BEHIND YOU!

December 4

For My Friends Who Have Messed Up: If you have messed up or FAILED in any way please don't give up on yourself or on the Lord.

December 5

I've learned in my own life and from the lives of many others that FAILURES will either make you BITTER or BETTER.

December 6

The only difference between "bitter" and "better" is the letter "I" – I make the difference. In other words, it's YOUR choice NOT to give up.

December 7

You can't learn from your mistakes if you keep denying you made them. Be humble!

December 8

It's time 2...GET OVER IT!!! and GET ON WITH IT!!!

December 9

Sometimes the only way to get CLOSURE is to stop being OPEN to further conversations!

December 10

Friends, don't cry over the PAST, it's gone. Don't stress about the FUTURE cause it hasn't arrived. Live in the present and make it beautiful.

December 11

We don't need to rush. If something's bound to happen, it will happen. In the right time, with the right person, for the best reason.

December 12

If two people are meant to be together, eventually they'll find their way back. Being faithful to your partner should be common sense.

December 13

You can't have a
relationship
without any fights,
but you can make
your relationship
worth the fight.

December 14

BEFORE you decide to get married: If you are in a dating relationship and you feel like you are being TOLERATED & not CELEBRATED perhaps it's time to move on.

December 15

Love doesn't always have a happy ending. Just because you love someone so much, doesn't mean they are the right one for you.

December 16

You may not be the girl that EVERYONE WANTS but at least you are not the one that EVERYBODY HAS HAD! *Psalm 139:14 I am fearfully & wonderfully made!*

December 17

Listen to me with both ears: Certain guys will tell you ANYTHING to get in between your legs. Its called LUST not LOVE. Don't get it twisted.

December 18

If a guy can't handle you in sweat pants, he surely doesn't deserve you in a wedding dress!
–Drake

December 19

For My Friends Who Feel Manipulated: If certain people resent u 4 doing what is best 4 u then they were never concerned about u only what u could do 4 them. #OpenYourEyes

December 20

#UnspokenTruth
Ladies: When a man
is proud of the
relationship he's in,
he will tell the world!
When he's not, he'll
claim to be a "private
person".

December 21

Friends, please don't let your past HURTS make you cynical about being currently HAPPY!

December 22

You meet people
for a reason, either
they're a blessing
or a lesson!

December 23

Drama does not just walk into your life. You either create it, invite it, or associate with people who love to bring it into your life.
#ChangeItUp

December 24

If you want to
know your past,
look into your
present conditions.
If you want to
know your future,
look into your
present actions.

December 25

I can do everything through Him who strengthens me.
Philippians 4:13

God wants you to know that you have everything you need to succeed because he will give you the strength to do absolutely anything he asks!

December 26

Do not let the behavior of others destroy your inner peace.

December 27

To judge someone on their looks is to judge yourself on character... LOVE EVERYONE!

December 28

There comes a time in your life, when you walk away from all the drama and people who create it. You surround yourself with people who make you laugh. Forget the bad and focus on the good. Love the people who treat you right, pray for the ones who don't. Life is too short to be anything but happy. Falling down is a part of life, getting back up is living!

December 29

Whether you think you can, or think you can't, you're probably right!

December 30

Never say 'I can't'.
Always say, 'I'll
try.' Even better,
say... 'I WILL!'

December 31

"If you want the rainbow, you got to put up with the rain. Remember that it can't storm forever and the clouds will pass by. At the end of this, the sun will be shining down on you."

18154106R00231

Made in the USA
Middletown, DE
24 February 2015